WHOLE FOOD

60 Recipes of Complete Whole Food Diet to a Total 30 Day Transformation

The Whole Food 30 Diet Meal Plan Guide

30 Day Calendar Cookbook of Whole Foods

ALEX CLARK

ISBN-10: 1530493757
ISBN-13: 978-1530493753

CONTENTS

Introduction

Thank you for purchasing this book!

There are millions of diets plans everyday. What you choose and how you stick to it, matters the most! Modern living has certainly changed the lifestyles, however, the body still functions as it used to, since always. When you decide to hear what the body needs and how it can stay healthy, you look out for all the options available.

The Whole Food Diet Plan, is a simple regime that does not push you to lose weight. Instead, it guides you to cleanse and rejuvenate your body from within, subsequently helping you lose weight and enjoy lasting energy. All you need to do is look back and incorporate the food lifestyle of the ancestors, who ate nothing but healthy natural food. With no "processed food" in sight, they survived on raw vegetables, meats and other non-processed items that were dense in nutrients, that cut-down cravings and are easily digestible. This Whole Food Diet Plan is one solid step toward achieving a healthy lifestyle. It is a comprehensive diet plan with its own set of rules. So, no calorie counting, no complex juices and no losing motivation. All you do is eat 3 simple and delicious whole meals that satisfy your hunger and nourish your body!

This book is a guide on the basic principles of the Whole Food Diet Plan. It contains a 30-Day Meal Plan as well as 60 healthy and delicious recipes for your breakfast, lunch, dinner and snacks. You can tweak the plan and cook as you desire. Once the 30 days are over, you would not wish to go back to processed food again!

So, take a break, reset your body, change your food habits and enjoy the Whole Food Diet!

1 Chapter 1: The Whole Food Diet Plan for 30 Days

The Whole Food Diet includes foods that are unprocessed and unrefined, in its most natural state before being consumed. It's a diet that is based on fruits, vegetables, whole grains, legumes and lean low-fat meats. There are numerous health benefits for consuming whole foods as it prevents diseases, increases energy levels, lowers the cholesterols, reduces stress and improves your health. The best part is unlike the other diets, the Whole Food Diet can change your natural cravings and affect the way you view diet on a long term basis. It brings the body to a metabolic state where you burn fat for energy, instead of glucose and carbohydrates. It is certainly a delicious way to lose weight as well.

30 Whole Food Recipes for 30 Days

Day 1: Recipe # 1: Coconut Pancakes

Ingredients:

4 Eggs

2 Ripe Bananas

½ cup Coconut flour

3 tbsp. Coconut sugar

1 tbsp. Coconut oil

1 tsp. Baking soda

½ tsp. Ground cinnamon

Instructions:

1. Whisk the eggs in a bowl. Add the rest of the ingredients to form a smooth batter.

2. Heat a pan and melt half coconut oil.

3. Ladle a scoopful of the mixture.

4. Cook until bubbles appear and then flip. Cook well on both sides. Serve immediately.

Day 2: Recipe # 2: Spicy Squash Soup

Ingredients:

1 (2 lb.) Butternut squash, cubed

2 Carrots, medium, chopped

1 White onion, medium, chopped

1 Apple, medium, chopped

2 tbsp. Ground cinnamon

1 tsp. Ground chipotle pepper

1 tsp. Ground cumin

Fresh cilantro, for garnish

Instructions:

1. Preheat the oven to 375 degrees F. Combine the squash, carrots, apple and onion on a large rimmed baking sheet. Sprinkle cinnamon and cumin and toss to mix together. Apple a splash of water and place it in the oven to roast. Leave it for 45 minutes.

2. Take out the veggies and place them in a large soup pot with 5 cups water and group chipotle.

3. Bring to a boil and leave to simmer until the squash is tender. Use a blender to puree the mix. Serve hot with a handful of cilantro.

Day 3: Recipe # 3: Greek Chicken Salad

Ingredients:

3 cups Chicken breast, cooked and shredded

2 tbsp. Kalamata olives, pitted and chopped

¾ cup Plain yogurt

¾ cup Cherry tomatoes, halved

½ cup Mayonnaise

1 tsp. Fresh oregano

1 cup Cucumber, diced

3 Cloves garlic, finely chopped

½ cup Crumbled feta

¼ cup Fresh Italian parsley, chopped

Instructions:

1. In a large bowl mix the yogurt, mayonnaise, garlic and oregano. Mix well until the texture is creamy.

2. Add chicken, tomato, cucumber, olives, feta and parsley and toss well.

3. Place the salad in the refrigerator for 30-60 minutes and serve on lettuce leaves or in sandwiches.

Day 4: Recipe # 4: Crunchy Chicken Nuggets
Ingredients:

Cooking spray

1 lb. Chicken breasts, boneless, skinless, cut into 2-inch chunks

½ cup Plain yogurt

2 cups Cornflakes, crushed

2 tbsp. Parsley, chopped

½ tsp. Freshly ground white pepper

½ tsp. Salt

½ cup Honey mustard sauce for dipping

Instructions:

1. Place the chicken chunks with yogurt in a medium bowl and let it marinate for an hour or overnight.

2. Preheat oven to 375 degrees F. Take a baking sheet. Grease with cooking spray.

3. Place corn flakes, parsley, salt and pepper in a large reseal able plastic bag and mix them well by shaking. Drop the chicken pieces

into the bag, few pieces at a time. Seal and shake to coat and then place the chicken into the baking sheet.

4. Bake the chicken for 20-25 minutes until they are crunchy on the outside and tender in the inside.

5. Serve with honey mustard sauce for dipping.

Day 5: Recipe # 5: Black Pepper Roast Beef with a Honey Glaze

Ingredients:

1 (4 lbs.) Beef top round roast

2 tbsp. Black pepper, coarsely ground

1 tbsp. Coarse sea salt

6 tbsp. Honey

3 tbsp. Balsamic vinegar

1 tbsp. Canola oil, expeller-pressed

Instructions:

1. Preheat the oven to 400 degrees F. Rub salt and pepper all over the beef. Place the beef on a rack fitted into roasting pan. Roast for 45 minutes.

2. In a medium bowl, whisk together honey, vinegar, and oil. After 45 minutes of roasting beef, use a brush and apply the honey mixture all over the beef. Cook for 15 more minutes, and then reduce oven temp to 350 degrees.

3. Insert a thermometer in the beef to check if the thick part reads

125 degrees for medium rare. Keep brushing with honey glaze every 15 minutes and roast some more.

4. Place the roast on the cutting board, tent with a foil and let it rest for 15 minutes before slicing. This increases internal temp by 5 to 10 degrees.

5. Serve with the pan juices drizzled over top.

Day 6: Recipe # 6: Fish Fingers

Ingredients:

2 lbs. Cod fillets

2 ½ cups Breadcrumbs (gluten-free)

¼ cup Rice milk

1 tsp. Garlic powder

¼ tsp. Paprika powder

½ tsp. Onion powder

Salt and pepper to taste

Olive oil for frying

Instructions:

1. Marinate the fillets with milk, onion powder, garlic powder, paprika, salt and pepper for a few hours.

2. Once done, roll the fish fillets into the breadcrumbs.

3. Heat oil in a pan and deep fry the fish fillets. Don't overcrowd the pan.

4. Serve hot with a dip you wish.

Day 7: Recipe # 7: Veggies and Tofu Stir Fry

Ingredients:

1 ½ cup Cooked brown rice

14 oz. Extra firm tofu

2 cups Carrots, shredded

1 cup Bell peppers, sliced

1 cup Asparagus, chopped

½ cup packed Kale

2 minced Garlic cloves

2 tbsp. Olive oil

Salt and pepper to taste

Instructions:

1. Heat oil in a pan and fry garlic until golden. Add the tofu and stir-fry until golden brown.

2. Add the veggies and fry until they are tender but intact.

3. Season well and serve with brown rice.

Day 8: Recipe # 8: Rosemary Lamb Chops

Ingredients:

6 Lamb chops

2 Garlic cloves, minced

2 tbsp. Lemon juice

3 tbsp. Fresh rosemary, chopped

Salt and pepper to taste

2 tbsp. Olive oil

Instructions:

1. Marinate the lamb chops with seasonings for a few hours.

2. Preheat the oven to 350 degrees F.

3. Grease baking pan and place the lamb on them. Bake for 30 minutes to 45 minutes.

4. Flip the chops halfway through baking process.

5. Serve hot.

Day 9: Recipe # 9: Chicken and Cabbage Salad

Ingredients:

1 Chicken breast, cooked and cubed

2 cups Cabbage, sliced

2 tbsp. Cilantro, chopped

½ tbsp. Ginger shredded finely, browned

½ tbsp. Garlic, minced finely, chopped

1 tbsp. Rice vinegar

1 tbsp. Olive oil

Salt and pepper to taste

Instructions:

1. Toss all the ingredients together in a large bowl.

2. Serve.

Day 10: Recipe # 10: Lentil Chili

Ingredients:

2 ¼ cups Brown lentils

3 cups Diced tomatoes

8 cups Low-sodium vegetable broth, divided

2 tbsp. Olive oil

1 Yellow onion, medium, chopped

1 Red bell pepper, large, chopped

5 Garlic cloves, finely chopped

4 tsp. Salt-free chili powder

¼ cup Fresh cilantro, chopped

Instructions:

1. Heat a large pot. Put the oil and add onion, bell pepper and cook until the veggies turn brown and begin to stick to the bottom. Stir in about 3 tablespoons of broth and continue to cook until onion are soft and slightly browned.

2. Add the garlic and chili powder and stir constantly.

3. Add lentils, tomatoes and the rest of the broth. Boil the mix and reduce heat and simmer for 30 minutes until lentils are tender.

4. Uncover and cook for 30 minutes more. Stir in cilantro and serve.

Day 11: Recipe # 11: Shrimp and Mango Ceviche
Ingredients:

¾ lbs. Shrimps, medium, peeled and deveined

1 Mango, large, peeled, pitted and chopped

½ cup Red onion, finely chopped

¼ cup Cilantro, roughly chopped

6 tbsp. Lime juice

1 Tomato, chopped

1 Jalapeño pepper, seeded and finely chopped

¾ tsp. Fine sea salt

Instructions:

1. Bring a pot of water, generously salted, to a boil. Add the shrimps and cook for about a minute or 2, until they are pink and done. Drain and rinse under cold water. Drain excess water.

2. Chop the shrimps into ½ inch pieces. Place them in a large bowl and add onion, cilantro, lime juice, tomato, mango, jalapeño, and salt. Toss well, Cover and refrigerate for an hour. Serve cold.

Day 12: Recipe # 12: Chickpea and Spinach Omelette

Ingredients:

2 cups Chickpea flour

3 cups Baby Spinach

½ cup Yeast

2 tbsp. Flaxseeds

2 tsp. Turmeric

2 tsp. Baking soda

1 tsp. Garlic powder

Salt to taste

Instructions:

1. Cut the spinach finely and set aside.

2. In a large bowl, mix all the ingredients together (except spinach) and add a little water.

3. Make a smooth batter which is neither too thick nor too runny. Add the spinach to the mix.

4. Heat a non-stick pan and ladle a scoop of batter. Wait till one side

become done. Then flip it over. Cook until done and serve immediately.

Day 13: Recipe # 13: Thai Shrimp and Carrot Salad

Ingredients:

8 oz. Uncooked brown rice noodles

½ pound peeled, deveined and cooked medium shrimps (tails removed)

¼ cup Lime juice

¼ cup Rice vinegar

3 cups Shredded carrots

1/8 tbsp. Red chili pepper (crushed)

½ cup Unsalted peanuts (dry roasted)

½ cups Shallots (sliced)

½ cup Fresh mint (chopped)

Instructions:

1. Cook noodles as per the instructions in the package. Rinse, cool, drain and place in large bowl.

2. In another bowl, mix the lime juice, vinegar and crushed pepper to make the dressing. Toss 2 tablespoons of it on the noodles and mix.

3. The remaining dressing can be used with the shrimp, shallots, carrots, peanuts and mint. Serve this shrimp mixture over the rice noodles.

Day 14: Recipe # 14: Roasted Brussel Sprouts with Bacon and Walnuts

Ingredients:

3 slices Thick-cut bacon, sliced into 1/2-inch wide strips

2 lbs. Brussels sprouts, halved

½ cup Walnuts, toasted and chopped

¼ tsp Ground black pepper

¼ tsp. Fine sea salt

1 tsp. Fresh thyme, chopped

Instructions:

1. Preheat the oven to 400°F.

2. In an oven-proof skillet, cook the bacon until they are crispy. Move the bacon to the paper towel lined plate.

3. In the same skillet, add the sprouts, salt and pepper and toss till you combine them. Then place the skillet in the oven and roast the sprouts until they are deep golden brown, crispy outside and cooked inside. Stir occasionally.

4. Move the sprouts to a serving dish and toss in the bacon, walnuts

and thyme. Serve.

Day 15: Recipe # 15: Chicken Sausage with Cauliflower and Red Lentils

Ingredients:

1 tbsp. Canola oil

1 (12 oz.) pack of Cilantro chicken sausage, cooked and sliced

1 cup Red lentils, rinsed and drained

1 (16 oz.) pack of Frozen cauliflower, defrosted and drained

1 tbsp. Brown mustard seeds

2 cups Low-sodium chicken broth

1 ¾ cups Fresh tomatoes (chopped)

1 tsp. Fine sea salt

Instructions:

1. Heat oil in a large pan and add the sausage and cook until browned. Stir occasionally. Transfer to plate and set aside.

2. Now place the pan over heat and add mustard seeds and toast for 30 seconds. Add broth and scrape any brown bits.

3. Then add the cauliflowers and lentils and bring to a boil. Reduce

heat to medium-low, cover and let simmer until the liquid is absorbed.

4. Add the tomatoes and simmer until mixture is creamy and lentils are tender.

5. Add salt to taste. Toss in the browned sausage and serve.

Day 16: Recipe # 16: Devilled Eggs with Avocado-Lime

Ingredients:

3 hard-boiled eggs

½ Ripe avocado

½ Lime

1 tsp. Sriracha/any hot sauce

Dash of chipotle seasoning

Dash of celery salt

Salt and pepper to taste

Instructions:

1. Peel the eggs and slice them lengthwise

2. Remove the yolks and place in a bowl with sliced avocado. Smash them both to make a smooth paste.

3. Add the juice of the lime, hot sauce, chipotle seasoning and celery salt and mix well. Season with salt and pepper.

4. Spoon the yolk mixture back into the egg halves.

5. Serve with a sprinkle of chipotle.

Day 17: Recipe # 17: Egg and Salmon Canapé

Ingredients:

4 Gluten free crackers

4 pieces Smoked salmon

1 Hard-boiled egg, chopped

2 tbsp. Coconut cream

1 tbsp. Chives, chopped

1 tbsp. Parsley, chopped

Salt and pepper to taste

Instructions:

1. In a bowl, mix the egg, coconut cream, parsley, chives, salt and pepper.

2. On each cracker place this mixture along with a smoked salmon piece on top.

3. Serve immediately.

Day 18: Recipe # 18: Burritos

Ingredients:

3 Baked potatoes, cubed

4-6 Whole wheat tortillas

1 Sweet onion, chopped

1 Red pepper, chopped

½ Bunch kale, chopped

1 tbsp. Olive oil

Avocado, sliced

Tofutti cream and fresh salsa for dressing

Salt to taste

Instructions:

1. Heat oil in a pan. Add the onions and pepper and cook them for few minutes. Then add the baked potatoes and cook until they are crispy. Add salt to taste.

2. Remove pan from flame. Add the chopped kale to the cooked veggies and cover the lid for 2-3 minutes. This will steam the kale.

3. Use another pan and heat the tortillas on both sides. Scoop the veggies in the middle of the tortillas and top with Tofutti cream, avocado and fresh salsa. Serve.

Day 19: Recipe # 19: Turkey Sausages

Ingredients:

1 ½ lb. Ground turkey

2 Apples, medium, peeled and grated. Squeeze out the excess liquid.

2 Eggs, beaten

½ cup Parsley, chopped

3 tbsp. Fresh sage, finely chopped

½ tsp. Ground nutmeg

½ tsp. Ground black pepper

1 ½ tsp. Salt

Instructions:

1. Preheat the oven to 350 degrees F.

2. Mix the turkey, apples, eggs, parsley, sage, nutmeg, salt and pepper in a large bowl.

3. With a damp hand, shape the sausage mixture to make 8 patties.

4. In a non-stick skillet, brush some oil and heat.

5. Place the patties and brown them. Place the browned patties to the baking sheet and bake in the oven for 10 minutes until they are cooked through.

6. Serve.

Day 20: Recipe # 20: Coconut Pumpkin Butter with Toast

Ingredients:

1 cup Pumpkin puree

1 cup Coconut butter

3 tbsp. Maple syrup

1 ½ tsp. Cinnamon (ground)

1/8 Nutmeg (ground)

Salt to taste

4 Gluten free toasts

Instructions:

1. Combine all the ingredient together and mix well.

2. Spread the mix on a gluten free toast. Serve.

3. The mix can be refrigerated for a week as well.

Day 21: Recipe # 21: Mixed Grilled Vegetables

Ingredients:

½ cup Sweet bell peppers, quartered

½ cup Hot peppers, whole or cut in half

½ cup Zucchini and summer squash, cut into small planks

½ cup Mushrooms, whole/sliced

½ cup Onions, sliced

2 Tomatoes, whole

½ cup Corn, cleaned and cut or whole

1 Lime juice

Instructions:

1. Prepare the vegetables and then brush them with olive oil.

2. Cook them on a clean hot grill until they are crisp and tender for about 8-10 minutes.

3. Serve hot with a sprinkle of lime juice.

Day 22: Recipe # 22: Salsa Halibut

Ingredients:

4 Halibut fillets

1 tbsp. Olive oil

2 Tomatoes, diced

2 Garlic cloves, minced

1 tsp. Fresh oregano, chopped

2 tbsp. Fresh basil, chopped

Instructions:

1. In a bowl, combine the olive oil, oregano, garlic and basil.

2. Coat all the fillets with this mixture.

3. Place the fillets on a baking sheet that's pre-oiled and pour the diced tomatoes on top.

4. Bake for 10-15 minutes at 350 degrees F.

5. Serve with a dip of your choice.

Day 23: Recipe # 23: Easy Garlic Green Beans

Ingredients:

2 cups Frozen green beans

1 tbsp. Olive oil

1 tsp. Chopped garlic

1/4 cup water

Salt and pepper to taste

Instructions:

1. Take water in a large pan with a lid and add the beans to it. Steam cook the beans for 5 to 7 minutes, until tender. Drain the remaining water. Keep aside.

2. In a pan, add the oil along with the garlic. Stir in the beans until evenly distributed. Heat well for 10 minutes until the beans are well cooked and lightly browned.

3. Season with salt and pepper.

Day 24: Recipe # 24: Chicken-Fried Steak with Gravy
Ingredients:

1 ½ lbs. Beef cube steak/minute steak

¾ cup Almond flour/all-purpose flour

¼ tsp. of each (Pepper, garlic powder, onion powder, and mustard seeds)

Oil for frying

1 tsp. Salt

Gravy base

For Chicken Cream Soup

1 ½ cup Chicken broth

1 ½ cup Milk

½ tsp. Poultry seasoning

¼ tsp. Onion and garlic powder each

¼ tsp. Parsley, finely chopped

Salt and pepper

Dash of paprika

¾ cup Flour

Instructions:

1. Heat oil over medium flame.

2. In a reseal able bag, mix the flour, salt, pepper, onion powder, garlic powder, and dry mustard. Shake well.

3. Scour steaks in flour mixture.

4. Fry and flip until you get the desired brownness.

5. Place it on paper-towel lined plate. Keep it hot.

6. For the chicken cream soup, boil the chicken broth, 1/2 cup milk and seasonings for a minute or two. In a separate bowl, add the remaining milk and flour and make a smooth batter. Add this to the broth and stir constantly until mixture boils and thickens. This will make 2 cans of cream chicken soup.

7. Make a gravy base. Use cream chicken soup as a topping for the gravy.

8. Serve steaks along with mashed potatoes and gravy.

Day 25: Recipe # 25: Chicken and Cheese Tostadas
Ingredients:

3 cups Chicken, cooked and diced

1½ cups Monterey Jack cheese, freshly grated

1 Jalapeño finely diced

1½ Limes

8 Whole-grain 5" to 6" corn tortillas

2 tbsp. Water

1 tsp. Cumin

¼ tsp. Chili powder

½ tsp. Salt

Toppings: Sour cream, avocado and cilantro

Instructions:

1. Preheat the oven up to 450 degrees F.

2. Combine the chicken, cheese, water, spices, jalapeño and juice of 1 lime in a large bowl.

3. Lay the tortillas out on a large baking sheet, in one even layer. It depends on the baking sheet as to how many batches are made.

4. Evenly distribute the chicken mixture on top of the 8 tortillas and bake for 12-13 minutes until cheese begins to brown.

5. Squeeze the remaining ½ lime on top of the cooked tostadas.

6. Serve warm with sour cream, diced avocado, and cilantro.

Day 26: Recipe # 26: Baby Calamari with Garlic

Ingredients:

1 ½ lbs. of baby squid/calamari with heads, cleaned and pat dried

3 tbsp. Olive oil

1 Garlic head, minced

Red pepper flakes to taste

Sea salt

Cilantro for garnishing

Instructions:

1. In a pan, place the olive oil and sauté the calamari (and calamari heads) for 5-7 minutes, turning a few times.

2. Add the minced garlic and pepper. Cook for some more time till garlic becomes golden.

3. Add sea salt and season. Garnish with cilantro and serve.

Day 27: Recipe # 27: Thai Rice

Ingredients:

2 cups Brown rice

1 tbsp. Coconut oil

3 Garlic cloves, minced

1 tbsp. Chopped ginger

1 tbsp. Soy sauce without MSG

1 cup Cilantro, chopped

Salt

Instructions:

1. Heat oil in a pan and add the ginger and garlic. Cook until the garlic smell goes away.

2. Add rice and stir so it is evenly coated. Add water, fish sauce, and salt. Reduce heat and simmer for 20 minutes.

3. Once rice is cooked, sprinkle cilantro and taste for seasoning.

4. Serve the warm rice.

Day 28: Recipe # 28: Beef with Eggplant Stew

Ingredients:

2 tbsp. Olive oil

3 lbs. Chuck roast, boneless, cut into 1-inch cube

2 cups Beef broth

2 cups Eggplant, peeled and diced

1 Onion, diced

2 cups Carrots, peeled and sliced

2 Bay leaves

3 Cloves garlic, minced

2 tsp. Dried thyme

2 tbsp. Flour

2 tbsp. Olive oil

Mashed potatoes - Prepared

Salt and pepper

Instructions:

1. In a large pan, heat oil. Add the beef cubes and cook until brown.

2. Add salt, pepper and slow cook.

3. Next, sauté the onion and garlic, until clear. Add flour, bay leaves, thyme and stir well.

4. Transfer the mixture of seasoned beef broth to slow cooker. Cook it for 4 hours on low flame.

5. Use additional olive oil to sauté the eggplant. Cook for 7-8 minutes.

6. Stir eggplant, carrots into the slow cooker and again cook for 2 hours.

7. Serve it over mashed potatoes.

Day 29: Recipe # 29: New York Classic Strip Steaks

Ingredients:

2 lbs. Strip steaks, (1 1/2-inch thick)

1 tbsp. Extra virgin olive oil, divided

2 Cloves garlic, lightly crushed

1 Lemon, cut into wedges

½ tsp. Ground black pepper, divided

Instructions:

1. Prepare a grill on medium-high heat.

2. Season the steaks with salt and pepper on both sides. Then place the steaks on the grills and cook for 3 minutes.

3. Then rotate the steaks to 90 degrees and cook for 3 minutes more. This will give a nice grill mark.

4. Flip the steaks and repeat this grilling and rotating method until cooked. Check with a thermometer if the steaks have reached 145 degrees F for medium rare. Cook as you desire.

5. Transfer steak to a plate and wait for 5 minutes. Rub with garlic, drizzle with oil and serve with lemon wedges.

Day 30: Recipe # 30: Spaghetti Squash Pasta

Ingredients:

3 cups Brussels sprouts, trimmed

1 Spaghetti squash

½ cup Vegetable broth

1 Yellow onion, diced

2 tsp. Garlic, minced

½ tsp. Chili powder

Salt to taste

Instructions:

1. Boil the squash in water for 15 minutes.

2. In a separate skillet, add the broth, onions, garlic and Brussels sprouts and cook for 5 minutes.

3. Add the seasonings and spaghetti squash.

4. Cook until broth has dried.

5. Serve hot.

2 Chapter 2: What to Eat and What to Miss

The Whole Food Diet Plan was started with a few general ground rules. Let's start with the foods that need to be avoided. Strictly. For the first 30 days avoid using them at all. This will improve your metabolism and keep you on the right path.

Foods to Miss

1. No sugar: Omit sugar completely! They just increase problems, like diabetes and stress level. Sugar and all its variables should be completely avoided.

2. No artificial flavorings: This usually contains sugar and when you use it, it comes into your diet. Also, artificial coloring can be bad for health. So better to avoid them.

3. No dairy products: Try avoiding ice-creams and other dairy products. The exception is clarified butter or ghee that can be included. If must, you can also have a maximum of 2 cups of 1% or ½ % milk every day, very low-fat milk, low-fat sugar-free yogurt, sugar-free frozen yogurt, or sugar-free ice cream.

4. No alcohol: No beers, no light spirits, no drinks. Period. Don't use alcohol for cooking as well. Just cut them out.

5. No gluten: Most grain will be off-limits during this time. However, there are a few gluten-free grains that can be eaten.

6. No processed foods: Thinking of fruit juices, candies, cookies etc.! Well stop. The processed foods have crept into our daily life and taken hold of it. It is time to shrug them off and focus only of fresh natural foods. So flip the packet, and read the ingredients. Chuck out things that are processed or factory made.

The Not-Permitted Food List

1. Vegetables: Potatoes

2. Grains: White, polished grains, rye, barley, wheat, and oats

3. Proteins: Processed meat

4. Dairy: Cheese, unclarified butter, margarine, cow/goat milk

5. Seeds and nuts: Peanuts

6. Flavorings: MSG, soy sauce, artificial fruit essence, malt vinegar

Limit Yourself

1. Fruit Juices: In limited quantities, you can have the fruit juice that is fresh and homemade. Not the ones in cartons.

2. Salt: Use little salt in food. Best options are sea salt, Kosher salt, and pink Himalayan salt.

3. Restrict outside food: Don't eat out too often. If you have to eat out sometimes, make intelligent choices from the menu.

4. Bakery goods: Especially the bread and all, make sure if they say multigrain, it should be multi-grain with no sugars added. If you are not sure, bake your own bread.

5. Butter: Clarified butter is allowed. Don't use the yellow, regular butter as it may contain some milk proteins.

The Permitted Food-List

1. Salads and vegetables (non-starchy)

2. Whole fresh fruits (except bananas) and fruit that is canned or bottled without sugar.

3. Lean meat that includes poultry, duck, turkey, chicken, reduced-fat bacon like turkey bacon, lean ham, and reduced-fat sausages.

4. Egg whites

5. Fish, shrimps, crabs, prawns, beef, elk, buffalo, mutton, veal, turkey, soy

6. Reduced-fat cheese (chiefly cottage cheese)

7. Tea, coffee, and low-calorie juices

8. Seeds and nuts like almonds, walnuts, pistachios, pecans, pumpkin seeds, sunflower seeds, flax seeds.

9. Grain include millet, quinoa, corn, buckwheat and brown rice

10. Fats include olive oil, ghee, and coconut oil

11. Flavorings include maple syrup, herbs, spices, balsamic vinegar, apple cider vinegar, red wine vinegar, honey

12. Daily include rice milk, almond milk, coconut milk, clarified

butter and free range eggs

3 Chapter 3: Energizing Breakfast Recipes

Recipe # 1: Balsamic Blueberry Sandwich

Ingredients:

2 Gluten free multi-grain bread slices

½ cup Fresh blueberries

1 ½ tbsp. Maple syrup

1 tbsp. Balsamic vinegar

2 tbsp. Coconut cream

Instructions:

1. In a small saucepan, place the blueberries, balsamic vinegar and maple syrup.

2. Cook for 5 minutes and then drain the blueberries and set aside.

3. Layer the blueberries onto one bread slice and coconut cream onto

the other.

4. Close the sandwich and grill the bread until light brown. Serve.

Recipe # 2: Eggs with Basil Pesto
Ingredients:

12 eggs

1 yellow pepper, sliced whole in circles

1 red pepper, sliced whole in circles

Basil Pesto

Olive Oil

Instructions:

1. Use a large non-stick skillet and heat over medium heat.

2. Pour in a tablespoon of olive oil into the pan. Add the pepper rings and sauté for 1 minute.

3. Inside the pepper ring, crack and pour one egg and then place the cover on the pan.

4. Sauté the eggs for 2-3 minutes and serve with basil pesto.

Recipe # 3: Smoked Salmon Frittata

Ingredients:

3 - 4 oz. smoked salmon, sliced

4 large eggs, beaten with some water

½ tsp coconut oil or clarified butter/ghee

Sliced green onions for garnish

Ingredients:

For the green onion sauce

½ cup raw cashews

1 cup coconut milk

½ cup green onion chopped finely

1 tbsp. lemon juice

½ tsp. Garlic power

Salt and pepper to taste

Instructions for green onion sauce:

1. Ground the cashews in a blender till it is fine. Add coconut milk,

lemon juice, and garlic powder and blend till the mixture is thick and creamy.

2. Add the chopped green onions and season with salt and pepper.

3. Refrigerate to thicken the sauce.

Instructions:

1. Use a large skillet and add the oil or butter. Evenly coat the pan with oil.

2. Add the beaten eggs now

3. Preheat the broiler.

4. Cook the eggs till the end starts to pull away from the edges and the middle portion is still wet.

5. Now place the skillet under the broiler. Cook until the eggs are set, firm and springy when you touch

6. Now remove the pan from the broiler and slide the eggs into the plate.

7. Top with the sliced smoked salmon, with the chopped green onions. Liberally dress with onion sauce and serve.

Recipe # 4: Crab and Bacon Tacos

Ingredients:

4 Slices cooked bacon, crumbled

6 Eggs, beaten

½ tbsp. Bacon fat reserved

6 oz. Crab claw meat, drained

2 tbsp. Chives, chopped

4 Whole wheat tortillas, warmed

Instructions:

1. Use a pan and add the bacon fat. Cook the eggs in it and stir often for 2-3 minutes.

2. Add the crab and toss it gently for around 2 more minutes. Add the crumbled bacon as well.

3. Spoon them into tortillas and garnish them with chopped chives before serving.

Recipe # 5: Italian Roasted Chunky Potatoes

Ingredients:

2-3 lbs. Organic gold potatoes, cut into large chunks

4 tbsp. olive or avocado oil

2 tsp. Italian seasoning

salt to taste

Instructions:

1. Preheat the oven to 375 degrees.

2. Add all the ingredient and mix them in a large bowl. Pour them into a baking sheet in single layer.

3. Bake the potatoes for 30-35 minutes, until they are tender and golden brown. Serve.

Recipe # 6: Celery Root, Yam with Bacon Hash

Ingredients:

6-7 pieces of bacon, diced

1 celery root, peeled and cubed (1/2 inch)

1 large yam, peeled and cubes (1/2 inch)

½ large onion, diced

1-2 tbsp. ghee

1 tsp. smoked paprika

4 cloves garlic, minced

Sea salt and pepper

1-2 tbsp. fresh parsley, minced

Instructions:

1. Fill a pot with water and add a pinch of salt. Once it boils, add the cubed yams into the water. Cover and cook for 15 minutes till the yams are tender.

2. Once they are cooked, drain the water.

3. In a large sauté pan, cook the bacon pieces till they are crispy. Use

a slotted spoon and remove the bacon. Add the onions to the leftover bacon grease and sauté. Cook for 5 minutes till they are translucent.

4. Add the celery roots and cook till they are soft. It may absorb all the bacon grease so you may add the ghee to the mix so that the hash does not burn.

5. Once the celery roots are soft, add yams and garlic and cook till yams turn brown.

6. Season the hash with salt and pepper. Add the smoked paprika and bacon and mix gently.

7. Garnish with the chopped parsley and serve.

Recipe # 7: Kasha Porridge

Ingredients:

2 cups Water

1 cup Kasha

1 stick Cinnamon

1 tbsp. Maple syrup

1 pinch Salt

Instructions:

1. In a sauce, add the water and toss the cinnamon stick in. Bring to a boil.

2. Add the kasha and a bit of salt.

3. Reduce heat to low and cook for 15 mins.

4. Serve the porridge with maple syrup.

Recipe # 8: Chicken Tacos with Sweet and Mild Salsa
Ingredients:

2 Chicken breast halves, boneless and cooked

12 corn Tortillas

1 tbsp. Honey

1 jar Mild Green Salsa

½ cup crumbled Mexican cheese

Instructions:

1. In a skillet, heat the honey and salsa. Remove half of the salsa into a bowl.

2. Chop the chicken into chunks and add them to the rest of the salsa. Cook on medium heat for 5 minutes.

3. Warm the tortillas in a skillet and place them on plates. Then add 2 tablespoons of the chicken salsa and sprinkle some cheese.

4. Fold the tortillas into half and serve with salsa.

Recipe # 9: Skillet Poached Eggs with Leeks, Pea-Tendrils and Spinach

Ingredients:

2 tbsp. olive oil or salted butter

2 Eggs

2 cups Pea tendrils and spinach leaves

1/2 leek, sliced finely into half moons

Salt to taste

Freshly ground pepper, to taste

Instructions:

1. Take a small skillet and heat the butter or oil. Add the leek and sauté for 3-5 minutes till tender.

2. Now toss in the pea tendrils and spinach. Stir well until they wilt and then season with salt and pepper.

3. Take another pan and make a well using the greens. Crack an egg into this well and season well.

4. Cover until the egg is cooked as you desire and serve.

4 Chapter 4: Healthy Lunch Recipes

Recipe # 1: Vegetable Quesadilla

Ingredients:

Canola oil spray

1 cup Spinach leaves, sliced

½ cup Bell pepper, diced

1 Whole grain tortilla

¼ cup Salsa

¼ cup Mild Cheddar, shredded

Instructions:

1. Place a skillet on medium heat and coat it with the cooking spray

2. Add the bell peppers and sauté. Then add the spinach and cook till it is wilted and soft.

3. Push the veggies to one side and place the tortilla into another. Add cheese over half of the tortilla and then place the vegetable on top. Fold in half and cook until the bottom is brown. Carefully flip and cook the other side.

4. Place on cutting board and slice into wedges. Serve with salsa.

Recipe # 2: Chickpea Caesar Salad with Quick Chicken

Ingredients:

6 Chicken nuggets, cooked and chopped (leftovers work great)

1 Head romaine lettuce, chopped

¼ cup Caesar dressing

15 oz. Garbanzo beans, drained

Instructions:

1. Toss all the ingredients into a bowl.

2. Serve.

Recipe # 3: Arugula with Lemon, Steak, and Parmesan

Ingredients:

1 bunch Arugula

1 ½ lbs. Beef tri-tip

3 tbsp. Extra virgin olive oil

1 ¼ tbsp. Balsamic vinegar

2 ½ tbsp. Lemon juice

¾ cup Parmesan cheese, shaved

Salt and pepper to taste

Instructions:

1. Combine oil with salt and pepper and keep aside.

2. Grill the beef and let it cool for 10 minutes. Then slice it thinly.

3. In a bowl, toss in the arugula with the dressing. Place the beef slices and top it with parmesan. Serve.

Recipe # 4: Broccoli and Chicken

Ingredients:

2 lbs. Chicken, diced

7 cups Broccoli, diced

2 tbsp. toasted Sesame oil

2 tbsp. Ginger, grated

1 tsp. Salt

1 tsp. Garlic powder

1 tsp. Red pepper flakes

2/3 cup Coconut aminos

1 tbsp. Tapioca starch

Instructions:

1. Take a large skillet. Put the oil and then toss in the broccoli, ginger, garlic powder, red pepper flakes, coconut aminos, and salt.

2. Cook for a few minutes over medium heat until the broccoli softens a bit.

3. Add the chicken and turn flame to medium- high. Cook until the

chicken is cooked, stirring intermittently.

4. Add some tapioca starch and stir well until the sauce is thick.

5. Serve with noodles or cauliflower rice.

Recipe # 5: Lentil and Quinoa Salad with Cashews
Ingredients:

1 cup Quinoa

½ cup Green lentils, sprouted

2 tbsp. Dijon mustard

2 tbsp. Bragg liquid aminos

2 tbsp. Bragg sprinkle seasoning

2 tbsp. Red wine vinegar

2 cups Baby arugula

½ cup Red bell pepper, roasted and diced

¼ cup Cashews, toasted

1 Shallot, minced

1 Lemon, wedged

1 Fennel bulb, thinly sliced

Instructions:

1. Cook the lentils and quinoa in separate pans, as per directions.

Drain lentils and set them aside to cool.

2. In a bowl, add shallot, arugula and fennel bulb and whisk in the amino' s (all of them). Add the lentils, quinoa, and bell peppers, and mix.

3. Garnish with cashews and lemon wedges and serve.

Recipe # 6: Beef and Bone Marrow Soup

Ingredients:

1 pack Marrow bones (2-3 pounds)

1 pack Grass fed soup bones (2-3 pounds)

12 cups chopped vegetables (Use leafy greens, carrots, and rutabaga)

Filtered water

Instructions:

1. Place the marrow and soup bones in a large pot. Add the filtered water to the pot.

2. Boil the water and then reduce to simmer for 2-3 hours.

3. While the meat gets cooked, prepare the veggies.

4. When meat is done, remove bones from the broth and add the vegetables to the broth.

5. Cook in low flame for about 30 minutes. While this is cooking, remove meat, tissues and the marrows from the bone.

6. Shred the meat and set aside. Add any fat, marrow or connective tissues to the meat and bones to a blender.

7. Cover this with the broth and blend till smooth.

8. Add meat and the blended tissues to the cooked vegetables.

9. Serve hot.

Recipe # 7: Stuffed Avocado with Garlic Shrimp

Ingredients:

2 cups Shrimps (medium to large), raw and frozen - defrost before cooking.

1 whole Avocado, medium

Olive oil

5-6 cloves Garlic, minced

Salt

Ground pepper

Fresh parsley, chopped

Chili powder

Instructions:

1. Halve the avocado and remove the pit. Also, scrape out most of the meat and leave the shell with a thin layer. Keep aside

2. Chop up the meat and place in a bowl. Crush some with your fingertips. Keep aside.

3. In a medium pan, place 2 tablespoons of olive oil and toss in the

minced garlic and shrimps.

4. Add some salt and cook over low heat till the shrimps becomes moist and pink. Don't overcook as it may turn dry and hard.

5. Add the shrimps with the garlic and olive oil into the bowl with the avocado meat.

6. Add the chopped parsley and mix well. Add a pinch of chili powder to get a zing.

7. Now spoon the shrimp and avocado mixture into the avocado shells and garnish with pepper and parsley. Serve.

Recipe # 8: Orange Chicken Stir Fry

Ingredients:

2 Chicken breasts, diced

2 tbsp. Avocado oil

1 tbsp. Tamari soy sauce

1 navel Orange, peeled

4-5 cloves Garlic, peeled

1 tsp Fresh ginger

½ tsp. Salt

Instructions:

1. Take a pan and stir fry the chicken dices in the avocado oil. Add some salt to it.

2. Prepare the orange sauce by blending navel orange with ginger, garlic, and tamari sauce.

3. Once the chicken is tender and brown, add in half of the sauce.

4. Keep stirring until the sauce disappears.

5. Serve with sauce.

Recipe # 9: Creamy Red Curry Slaw

Ingredients:

2 cups Broccoli slaw

¼ cups Mayonnaise

1 tbsp. Thai kitchen red curry paste

1 Avocado, diced

½ cup Yellow bell pepper. chopped

Instructions:

1. In a bowl, toss in all the ingredients and serve.

2. You can eat them plain or with rice or in a gluten-free wrap.

5 Chapter 5: Sumptuous Dinner Recipes

Recipe # 1: Sautéed Shrimp and Couscous
Ingredients:

1 ½ lb. Shrimp, medium, peeled and deveined

8 cups. Baby field greens

1 tbsp. Extra virgin olive oil

2 cloves Garlic, minced

1 ½ tsp. Lemon juice

1/3 cup Italian vinaigrette dressing

1 ¼ cup Couscous, cooked

2 tbsp. Parmesan, grated

Salt and pepper to taste

Instructions:

1. Heat the olive oil in a skillet and sauté the shrimp and garlic over medium heat. Add salt and pepper to season them.

2. Cook for 5 minutes until the shrimps are done. Add lemon juice and stir.

3. Arrange the greens in a serving bowl and add the dressing. Toss them. Place the salad on serving plate, add the shrimps, couscous, and some cheese and serve.

Recipe #2: Spaghetti and Meatballs

Ingredients:

1 lb. Ground beef

2 cups Nomato sauce

4 Zucchini

½ Spaghetti squash

1 Onion, small, finely chopped

3 Garlic cloves, minced

1 tbsp. Fresh herbs

2 tbsp. Butter or Ghee

Instructions:

1. Cook the spaghetti squash and prepare the vegetable noodles. If you spiralize it, add a generous amount of salt and let it sit.

2. Take a bowl and mix the ground beef, garlic, onion and seasonings. Divide the mix into 15 meatballs.

3. Take a large pot and add 2 tablespoons of oil. Add the meatballs and cook them well so the outsides are brown.

4. Add the Nomato sauce and the other desired seasonings.

5. Cover and let it simmer for 10 minutes.

6. In the meantime, rinse the spiralized noodles well. Add the vegetable noodles to the pot and stir well.

7. Check if meatballs are booked and noodles done as per your taste. Serve hot.

8. For separate servings, you can sauté the noodles after rinsing them over medium heat until tender. Serve meatballs on top of noodles.

Recipe # 3: *Carrot and Potato Kugel*

Ingredients:

6 Potatoes, peeled and grated

4 Carrots, grated

3 Eggs, beaten

1 Onion, sliced, minced

6 tbsp. Matzo meal

2 tbsp. Parsley, chopped

Canola oil

1 ½ tsp. Paprika

¾ tsp. Black Pepper

1 ¾ tsp. Salt

Instructions:

1. Preheat the oven to 375-degree F.

2. In a bowl, mix the carrots, potatoes and onion and then add the eggs to the mix.

3. Stir in the Matzo meal, salt, pepper, and parsley and pour the mix into a baking pan that has been greased.

4. Use the entire content, sprinkle the top with paprika.

5. Bake for an hour till they are brown. Serve.

Recipe # 4: Cilantro Lime Halibut

Ingredients:

1.5-2 lbs. Halibut

1 cup Cilantro

2 Limes

½ cup Olive oil

3 tbsp. Olive oil separately for cooking

Salt and pepper to taste

Instructions:

1. Place all the ingredients except the fish and cooking oil in a blender and blend well.

2. Marinate the fish for 10-15 minutes, by placing them in a Ziploc bag and pouring in the cilantro mixture into it. Toss until the fishes are coated well.

3. In a skillet, add the 3 tbsp olive oil on medium heat. Add the halibuts and cook for 4-5 minutes each side. Serve.

Recipe # 5: Tofu and Black Bean Tacos

Ingredients:

1 pack Tofu, extra firm, drained

1 can Black beans, drained and rinsed

1 tbsp. Extra virgin olive oil

1 ½ tsp. Chili powder

½ tsp. of each (Dried oregano, Ground cumin, Ground coriander, Sea salt)

3 Green onions, minced

3 Cloves garlic, minced

12 Corn Tortillas, warmed

3 cups Green leaf lettuce, shredded

2 cups chopped tomatoes

1 ½ cup Cheddar cheese, shredded

Instructions:

1. Take a bowl and place the tofu. Mash it with a fork and add the chili powder, cumin, coriander, oregano and salt. Set aside.

2. In a skillet, heat oil and sauté the garlic and two-third green onions for 2 minutes.

3. Add tofu to the skillet and cook for 10 minutes. Stir well.

4. Add the beans and rest of the green onions and stir again for 2 minutes.

5. Spoon the tofu into the tortillas and top with lettuce, tomatoes, and cheese. Serve.

Recipe # 6: *Creamy Chicken Salad with Apples and Yogurt*

Ingredients:

1 lb. Chicken breast, skinless, diced, cooked

¾ cup Celery, minced

2 Green onions, minced

1 Apple, chopped

1 cup Cottage cheese

2 tsp. Lemon juice

1 tsp. Honey

1 tsp. Dijon mustard

2 tbsp. Plain yogurt

2 tbsp. Milk

Salt and pepper to taste

Instructions:

1. Place the chicken, celery, green onions and apple in a bowl and keep aside.

2. Put the cheese and all other ingredients in a blender and puree them until they are smooth.

3. Pour this mix on the bowl with chicken and apples and stir gently to coat.

4. Cover and chill until you serve.

Recipe # 7: Tangy Tuna Salad Sandwich

Ingredients:

6 slices Whole wheat sandwich bread

6 leaves of Butter lettuce

¼ cup Yogurt

¼ tsp. Curry powder

2 tbsp. Green onions, chopped

½ tsp. Lemon zest

1 tbsp. Dill, minced

¼ cup Celery, chopped

1 tbsp. Raisins, seedless

1 can Tuna

¼ tsp. Salt

Instructions:

1. Combine all the ingredients except for the bread and lettuce leaves and mix well. Refrigerate for half an hour.

2. Spread on the bread and top with lettuce leaves. Serve.

Recipe # 8: Roasted Monkfish and Tomatoes

Ingredients:

¾ lb. Monkfish fillets, skinless and boneless (sliced into medallions)

3 Roma tomatoes, sliced

1 ½ tsp. Extra virgin olive oil

½ tsp. Crushed red chili flakes

½ tsp Salt

¼ tsp. Pepper

Instructions:

1. Preheat the oven to 450-degree F. Line a baking sheet with some parchment paper.

2. Place the fishes and tomatoes to make two rows, slightly overlapping.

3. Season with salt and pepper and drizzle the olive oil on them.

4. Sprinkle the chili flakes and roast for 10-12 minutes without flipping. Serve.

Recipe # 9: Leg of Lamb with Roasted Fennel
Ingredients:

To Marinade

½ cup Orange juice

1/3 cup Olive oil

1 cup White wine

2 Lemon, juice and zest

2 Garlic cloves, chopped

¼ cup Mediterranean dried seasoning + reserve 1 tsp for gravy

2 tsp. Salt

6 lb. leg of lamb, boneless and tied

For Gravy

3 Fennel bulbs, quartered

2 tbsp. Vegetable oil

½ cup White wine

2 cups Chicken broth

2 tbsp. Flour with 2 tbsp. unsalted butter

Zest from 1 lemon

Salt and pepper to taste

Instructions:

For Marinade

1. To make the marinade, take a bowl and place the lamb legs into it.

2. Take the rest of the ingredients for marinade along with salt and pepper and blend into smooth paste.

3. Pour the paste into the lamb bowl and mix well. Refrigerate for a day.

4. When you plan to roast the lamb, take the bowl out and bring it to room temperature before roasting.

For the Roast

1. Preheat the oven to 450 degrees F. Toss the fennel into the oil and then place the fennel into the bottom of roasting pan. Now take the lambs out of the marinade and then place it on the roasting pan.

2. Discard remaining marinade. Pat the roast until it is dry. Brush it with olive oil and season with salt and pepper.

3. Place the lamb with the fat side facing the roasting rack. Roast for 20 minutes. Then reduce temperature to 300 degrees.

4. Roast for another hour and a half and stick in a thermometer to check if the middle portion of the lamb is 145 degrees.

5. Let it cool down for 20 minutes and then carve it and arrange with the roasted fennel on a serving platter.

For the Gravy

1. Heat the roasting pan on medium heat. Then stir in the wine and scrape the bottom of any drippings.

2. Add the chicken broth and the other spices. Then let it simmer for 5 minutes. Whisk in the flour and butter mixture into the gravy and cook for 2 minutes.

3. Add the lemon zest and salt and pepper to taste. Pour on the lamb. Serve hot.

Chapter 6: Yummy Snack Recipes

Recipe # 1: Creamy Garlic Broccoli

Ingredients:

3 ½ cups Broccoli florets

½ cup Creamy garlic hummus

Black pepper

Lemon juice to taste

Instructions:

1. Cook the broccoli florets. You can steam, boil, roast or grill them.

2. Now, in a bowl, toss the florets in garlic hummus and coat them.

3. Add lemon juice and black pepper on top before you serve.

Recipe # 2: Zucchini Hummus

Ingredients:

2 Zucchini, medium, peeled and chopped

½ cup Tahini

⅓ cup Olive oil

⅓ cup Lemon juice

1½ tsp. Cumin

3 Garlic cloves

Salt and pepper to taste

Instructions:

1. Combine all the ingredients in a blender and mix them until they are smooth.

2. Serve with crisp raw veggies like celery sticks, cucumber slices, carrots etc.

Recipe # 3: Kale Chips

Ingredients:

1 bunch Kale, washed and dried

2 tbsp. Olive oil

Salt to taste

Instructions:

1. Preheat oven to 300 degrees F.

2. Remove the center stems from the kale and tear or cut the leaves.

3. In a bowl, toss the kale and olive oil together. Sprinkle with salt.

4. On a baking sheet, spread the kale leaves and bake at 300 degrees F for 15 minutes or until crisp.

Conclusion

Thank you once again for purchasing this book!

The Whole Food Diet Plan has thousands of followers and is steadily gaining momentum. It does not force you to starve and count calories. It just eliminates the unhealthy food products from your diet that weaken your body and rob your energy! It certainly is a deliciously healthy way to nourish and pamper yourself.

This book will guide you on how to begin this Whole Food Diet Plan and stay motivated. There is a 30-Day Meal Plan for you along with 60 mouthwatering, delicious and healthy recipes that you can make for breakfast, lunch, dinner and snack-time.

Enjoy the beginning of the rest of your life with "Whole Foods". Get the apron on and start cooking!

Thank you and good luck! – Alex Clark

65970848R00064

Made in the USA
San Bernardino, CA
07 January 2018